POP CULTURE
BY THE NUMBERS

While the numbers published in this book are the result of careful research
using the best sources available, they are nonetheless approximations. It is
also important to remember that data changes over time, often very quickly.

Published by Tess Press, an imprint of
Black Dog & Leventhal Publishers, Inc.
151 West 19th Street
New York, NY 10011

Manufactured in the United States
Cover and interior design by Daberko Design

ISBN-13: 978-1-60376-105-5
Paperback ISBN-13: 978-1-60376-150-5
h g f e d c b a

POP CULTURE

BY DAVID HOFFMAN

BY THE NUMBERS

TABLE OF

CONTENTS

TABLE OF CONTENTS

100: wins in Ali's amateur career, out of 108 bouts

3: lineal heavyweight championships won by Ali (the only fighter to do so)

19: times Ali successfully defended his championship title

2: times Ali won back the heavyweight title after losing it

3 years, 2 months: total time Ali was stripped of his championship title and banned from the sport when, due to religious beliefs, he refused to be inducted into the Army to fight in Viet Nam

5: times *Ring Magazine* named Ali "Fighter of the Year"

15: rounds underdog Chuck Wepner lasted against Ali in 1975, a fight that Sylvester Stallone admitted was the inspiration for *Rocky*

22 million: meals Ali has provided, through charity work, to feed the world's hungry

BARBIE

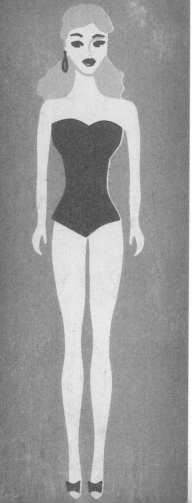

$3: original price of a Barbie doll in 1959

$10,000: highest amount paid to date for a #1 Barbie in mint condition

2: Barbie dolls sold every second, somewhere in the world

45: different nationalities Barbie has represented

80: careers Barbie has had since her first gig as an airline stewardess

5: sisters Barbie has (Skipper, Tutti, Stacie, Kelly, Krissy)

ONE BILLION SHOES

43 years: length of time Barbie dated Ken (from 1961 to 2004, at which point Mattel announced that the couple "feels it's time to spend some quality time–apart.")

1 billion: pairs of shoes Barbie has owned since 1959

105 million: yards of fabric used by Mattel to make Barbie fashions, making the toy company one of the largest apparel manufacturers in the world

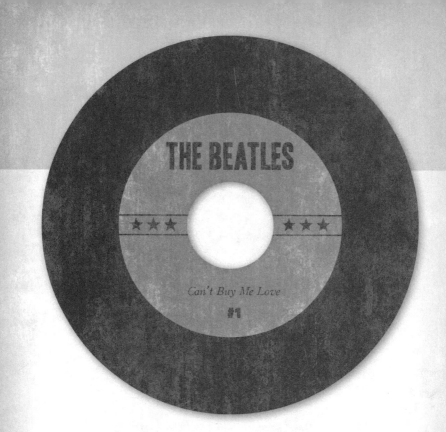

THE BEATLES

★ ★ ★   ★ ★ ★

Can't Buy Me Love

#1

$.01: royalty paid on each single sold in the U.K., per the Beatles' first recording contract in 1962 (it was split amongst the four of them)

5: number of positions, of the five top positions on the *Billboard* singles chart, occupied by the Beatles the week of April 4, 1964 ("Can't Buy Me Love" was #1)

75: million people that watched the Beatles television debut on *The Ed Sullivan Show* in 1964 (approximately half of the population of the U.S.)

28 minutes: length of the Beatles' performance at their August 15, 1965 concert at Shea Stadium

2,500: estimated number of covers of the Beatles' "Yesterday" (the most in pop history)

7: number of the Beatles' recordings on which only one Beatle performed all vocal and instrumental parts (Paul: "Yesterday", "Blackbird", "Her Majesty", "Mother Nature's Son"; John: "Julia"; Ringo: "Good Night"; George: "The Inner Light")

0: singles released off *St. Pepper's Lonely Hearts Club Band* (it was envisioned as a self-contained album meant to be played from start to finish)

0: times the name "the Beatles" was mentioned in the mock documentary *A Hard Day's Night*

150 million: copies of *Scouting for Boys: A Handbook for Instruction in Good Citizenship* published since 1908 (making it the 2nd best selling book of all time originally published in English, behind *A Tale of Two Cities*)

BOY SCOUTS

BRADY BUNCH
(1969-1974)

120: fields of skill and knowledge that are the basis of the merit badge program

5: percentage of Boy Scouts who earn the rank of Eagle Scout

2 years: how long it took noted human sexuality researcher Alfred Kinsey to earn the rank of Eagle Scout (versus the average time of 5 to 6 years)

15: age of director David Lynch when he became an Eagle Scout

88: age of the oldest person (Walter Hart of Fort Myers, FL) to ever become an Eagle Scout

of AMERICA

464: child actors auditioned by producer Sherwood Schwartz to play the Brady kids

34: the highest the series ranked in the Nielsen ratings (out of approximately 80 primetime programs) in the five seasons it ran

11: rooms (including attic) in the Brady's house

4: Brady kids who, at some point, wore braces (Marcia, Jan, Cindy and Bobby)

1: Brady kids who had a kissing scene (Bobby)

2: times the word "sex" was used in dialogue

0: questions Cindy got right when she appeared on "Quiz the Kids"

$56.23: cost of engraving the silver platter the Brady kids had bought as a gift for their parents' anniversary

BROADWAY

39:
Broadway theaters in
New York City

11.2 million: tickets to Broadway shows sold
annually

1: times an actor has appeared in two Broadway
shows simultaneously (In 1984, Cynthia Nixon co-
starred in both *Hurlyburly* and *The Real Thing*; she
would perform in the first act of one, in the second
act of the other, and then again in the third act of
the first)

0: Broadway shows depicted in the 42 theatre posters that line the walls of Joe Allen Restaurant in New York that were not major flops (meaning they ran less than a week or lost over a million dollars)

1300: caricatures on display at Sardi's restaurant

$50 to $100: amount in coins (mostly pennies) that is collected from the reflecting pool in front of the Vivian Beaumont Theater in Lincoln Center every two months (the money goes toward upkeep)

$76.32: average price paid for a ticket to a Broadway Show (2008)

BUDWEISER

800 years: duration that brewers in the town of Budweis (in what is today the Czech Republic) produced an eponymous style of larger called budweiser, before the drink was trademarked by Anheuser-Busch in the U.S. as a brand name

50.9: percentage of beer sold in the U.S. that is sold by Anheuser-Busch

10: percentage of annual U.S. rice crop purchased by Anheuser-Busch (Budweiser is one of the few beers that, in addition to barley, yeast, malt and hops, uses rice as an ingredient)

25,000: estimated size of crowd waiting outside the St. Louis Anheuser-Busch bottling plant at 12:01 a.m. on April 7, 1933, to buy beer, after the repeal of Prohibition

250: Clydesdale horses owned by Anheuser-Busch (the world's largest herd)

Campbell's

5: original flavors of Campbell's Soup (Tomato, Consommé, Vegetable, Chicken, and Oxtail)

8: average number of cans of Campbell's Soup found in an American home

216: average number of noodles in a can of Campbell's Chicken Noodle Soup

2: months per year (November, December) when Cream of Mushroom challenges perennial favorite Chicken Noodle as the number one selling Campbell's soup, thanks to its status as the main ingredient of the green bean casserole found on virtually every holiday table

70: cans of Campbell's Soup are sold every second in the U.S. (more than any other product in the supermarket)

32: soup cans (each representing a different variety) featured in Andy Warhol's painting *Campbell's Soup Cans*, which hangs in the Museum of Modern Art in New York, NY

$1000: price art dealer Irving Blum paid (in installments) to Andy Warhol in 1962 for his *Campbell's Soup Cans* painting

$11,776,000: price paid for Andy Warhol's *Small Torn Campbell's Soup Can (Pepper Pot)* at auction in 2006

88: ships currently in the Carnival fleet, making it the world's largest cruise line

475,250: shrimp ordered weekly to stock the buffet table on Carnival Cruise Lines' 22 Fun Ships (along with 108,140 pounds of chicken and 51,175 pounds of beef)

8 lbs.: average weight gain per person on a week-long cruise

2,781: gallons of fuel an average small cruise ship consumes per hour when traveling at a maximum speed of 24 knots

27: percentage of passengers on any given Carnival Cruise line that are senior citizens

20 years: length of time Kathie Lee Gifford crooned "If my friends could see me now . . ." as the spokesperson for Carnival Cruise Lines

52 years, 7 months: Cher's age when she hit the number 1 spot with "Believe" (1999), making her the oldest female recording artist to do so

4: consecutive decades (1960s–1990s) during which Cher has had a top ten hit single, making her the only recording artist to do so

5 years: length of time Cher wore braces (she had to keep taking them off every time she made a movie)

43 years: time to date that Bob Mackie has designed clothes for Cher (beginning in 1966, when she guest-starred on *The Carol Burnett Show*)

17: costume changes during "Cher at The Coliseum" at Caesars Palace in Las Vegas, one approximately every 5 minutes

2: times Cher topped Mr. Blackwell's "Worst Dressed List"

1941
CITIZEN KANE

$1 million: amount William Randolph Hearst offered RKO to destroy all prints of *Citizen Kane* and burn the negative

$60,500: price paid for the "Rosebud" sled in a 1982 auction at Sotheby's in New York (the winning bidder was Steven Spielberg)

2 weeks: length of time Orson Welles directed the film from a wheelchair, after chipping his anklebone while filming the scene where Kane chases Gettys down the stairs

01:32:46: point on the *Citizen Kane* DVD where, upon pausing the film, Jed Leland's scathing review of Susan's premiere performance can be read

24 hours: time Joseph Cotton stayed up in order to appear drunk in the scene where he decides to write the bad review

1: rank of *Citizen Kane* in the American Film Institute's list of the 100 Greatest American Movies of All Time

9: Coca-Cola fountain drinks sold per day in 1886 at Jacobs' Pharmacy in Atlanta, GA

3 million: Coca-Cola servings dispensed annually at the Varsity Drive-In Restaurant in Atlanta, GA (the highest volume of Coca-Cola served anywhere in the world)

7,000: Coca-Cola products consumed every second, somewhere in the world

200: countries where Coca-Cola is sold

$4 million: estimated cost of research to come up with the formula for New Coke in 1985

79 days: time it took for Coca-Cola to return original formula Coke to the shelves following the firestorm of protest over the introduction of New Coke

.0000000024: ounces of cocaine found in one gallon of Coca-Cola up until 1929 (according to scientists, not even enough to give a fly a buzz)

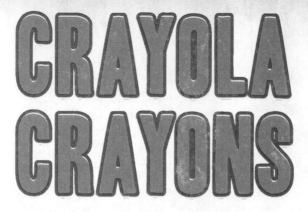

CRAYOLA CRAYONS

18: rank of Crayola crayons in a Yale University study of the top twenty most recognizable scents to American adults (coffee and peanut butter are #1 and #2)

8: colors available in the original Crayola box (the same 8 as today—black, brown, purple, blue, red, orange, yellow, green—although currently Crayola produces more than 120 colors)

23: variations of red currently available in the Crayola color line-up (the most shades of any color)

3: colors that have been renamed (due to political incorrectness) since their initial introduction —"prussian blue" to "midnight" (1958); "flesh" to "peach" (1962); and "indian red" to "chestnut" (1999)

28 minutes: average time per day that a child spends coloring

730: crayons the average child will have worn out by their tenth birthday

14: age of Grant Wood (*American Gothic*) when he won 3rd prize in a national Crayola drawing contest, which inspired him to become an artist

$250: price of a sculpture or commissioned portrait carved from a single Crayola Crayon by Seattle artist Diem Chau

THE DA VINCI CODE

1.5 million: increased annual attendance at the Louvre since 2005 (a fact most in the art world call the "The Da Vinci Code Effect"—attributing the increase in interest to Dan Brown's novel)

249: works by Leonardo da Vinci in the Louvre (more than you will find in Italy, or anyplace else)

673: diamond-shaped and triangular panes of glass in the Pyramid entrance to the Louvre (not 666, as commonly stated)

3 miles: distance Robert Langdon and Sophie Neveu would have traveled walking the perimeter of the Louvre

$105,000: original selling price of Mona Lisa (by today's economic standards)

$670,000,000: current estimated insured value of Mona Lisa

$47 million: value of the 133,000-square foot American Headquarters of Opus Dei in New York City

2: percentage of real-life Opus Dei members who are clergy (and none of them monks, according to the international Catholic organization)

$1: cost of admission on opening day in 1955

$69: current cost of admission (2009) for adults age 10 and older

78 million: number of pairs of Mickey Mouse ears that have been purchased since opening day and up until the park's 50th anniversary in 2005 (enough to adorn every child in America under 18)

land

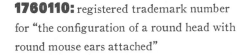

1760110: registered trademark number for "the configuration of a round head with round mouse ears attached"

30.3 mph: fastest speed reached on Space Mountain

99.9%: chance that the Monorail will arrive on time at any given stop

Disneyland

20,000: miles per year that the train on the Disneyland railroad travels, just by circling the park

8: vessels in the original Submarine Voyage, which when it opened in 1959, inadvertently made Walt Disney the commander of the 8th largest submarine fleet in the world

600: square footage of the apartment over Main Street Fire Station, where Walt Disney would occasionally stay when he visited the park

30: tons of garbage Disneyland generates in one day

1,850: tons of garbage Disneyland recycles yearly

$1: price of original Disney animation cels (once considered "worthless") when sold at the park's souvenir shops in the 1960s

$10,000: price paid by the Fujishige family, in 1954, for the 56 acres of strawberry fields across from Disneyland

$99.9 million: price paid by Disneyland, in the late 1990s, to the Fujishige family for 52.5 of the 56 acres

19 million: items available on the site at any given time (more than 300 times the number of units in a typical Wal-Mart)

1.8 billion: average number of items sold on eBay yearly (there are more transactions on eBay than on either the New York Stock Exchange or NASDAQ)

11 seconds: frequency in which a CD is sold on eBay

54: percentage of auction items listed that receive no bids

15: percentage of auction items that are won in the last minute

$14.83: winning bid for the very first item sold on eBay—a broken laser pointer

50 pence: "Buy It Now" price (approximately $1 U.S.) paid for the Lotus Esprit owned by British radio D.J. Tim Shaw (after his wife heard him flirting with a model on air, she listed the sports car and sold it within five minutes)

$85 million: the highest price paid to date for an item sold on eBay (and it wasn't even for the actual item, but for a 50% deposit on the item—a to-be-built 405-foot yacht)

EIFFEL TOWER

300: design proposals Gustave Eiffel beat out for the contract to build "an opening archway" to the 1889 Paris World's Fair

1063 feet: height of the Eiffel Tower

20: architectural replicas of the Eiffel Tower found around the world (ranging in height from 10 feet, in front of a construction company in Kazakhstan, to 540 feet, outside the Paris Hotel in Las Vegas)

200 million: visitors to the Eiffel Tower since its opening (the most of any paid admission tourist attraction in the world)

42 miles: distance visible, on a clear day and in every direction, from the top of the Eiffel Tower

20,000: bulbs currently illuminating the Eiffel Tower

2: number of times con man Victor Lustig successfully "sold" the Eiffel Tower to a scrap iron dealer

$108: average price of lunch at the Jules Verne restaurant on the second floor of the Eiffel Tower

15 months: time it takes to paint the Eiffel Tower, from start to finish

3: shades of a color used to paint the Eiffel Tower (lightest shade at the top, darkest at the bottom) to give it an even greater illusion of height

0: pennies thrown off the Empire State Building that have killed someone (and they won't; the building has an updraft so a coin dropped from the observation deck would be substantially slowed)

10 million: bricks in the Empire State Building

410: days it took to build the Empire State Building

45: seconds it takes to ride the elevator from the lobby to the 80th floor of the Empire State Building

9 minutes, 33 seconds: time it took Paul Crake (winner of the 2003 ESB Run-Up) to race up the 1,576 stairs leading from the lobby to the 86th floor of the Empire State Building (approximately 1/5th mile), the fastest time to date

4: months (from June–September, 1931) that the 102nd floor of the Empire State Building operated as an Air blimp terminal (the idea was quickly abandoned following several near disasters)

EMPIRE STATE

BUILDING

E.T. : The Extra

3 million : light years E.T. was from home

80: percentage increase Hershey Foods saw in sales of Reese's Pieces within two weeks of the film's initial release in 1982

10: percentage of the surprisingly low $10.5 million budget that went to build the full-size mechanical E.T., related animatronics, and the life-size E.T. costume

12: men it took to manipulate the full-size mechanical E.T.

4: actors who wore the E.T. costume (two dwarfs, a

Terrestrial (1982)

mime and a boy with no legs), although Spielberg's original idea had been to use a chimp on roller skates

3: famous faces whose features were combined to make E.T.'s face (Carl Sandburg's eyes, Albert Einstein's nose, and Ernest Hemingway's forehead)

1: adult faces seen in the first half of the film (Dee Wallace as Mary, the kids' mom)

$100,000: estimated cost Steven Spielberg spent to digitally remove guns from the film (the scene where the cops chase the kids and E.T. on their bikes) for its re-release in 2002 (they were replaced them with walkie-talkies)

facebook

2.6 billion: total minutes spent (worldwide) on Facebook daily

70%: Facebook users who are outside of the U.S.

2: countries that have banned access to Facebook (Syria and Iran)

13 million: users who update their status at least once daily

100: average "friends" for each individual user

$44,000: fine (in U.S. dollars) the High Court of London ordered Grant Raphael to pay for posting a fake Facebook page, charging him with invasion of privacy and defamation of character

FRIENDS (1994-2004)

18:

pages ("front and back") in the letter Rachel wrote to Ross, asking him to take responsibility for their first break-up (the letter that prompted him to say "We were on a break!" and prompted her to end their relationship)

3: nipples Chandler has

7: SISTERS JOEY HAS (VERONICA, MARY ANGELA, MARY THERESA, GINA, DINA, TINA, AND COOKIE)

255 LBS.: MONICA'S WEIGHT IN HIGH SCHOOL

11: categories of towels in neat-freak Monica's linen closet ("everyday use", "fancy", "guest", "fancy guest", etc)

THE GAP

1: number of clothing items the Gap originally offered (Levi's jeans) when it opened in 1969

3,100: current number of Gap stores (making it the world's second largest retailer, behind the Spanish clothing chain Zara)

308: celebrities who have been featured in Gap ad campaigns

15: pieces of fabric needed to make a standard pair of 5-pocket Gap jeans

15 minutes: time needed to make a standard pair of 5-pocket Gap jeans

2 seconds: time it takes to fold a short-sleeve t-shirt, if the Gap employee has been properly trained

GIRL SCOUT

2 million:
boxes of Girl Scout
Cookies sold annually

17,328: most boxes sold by a single
Girl Scout (Jennifer Sharpe of Dearborn, MI in
2008)

28: varieties of Girl Scout Cookies (not all are
available every year)

3: varieties of Girl Scout Cookies available every year, by order of the national organization of Girl Scouts (Thin Mints, Peanut Butter Sandwiches, and Shortbreads)

3: rank of Thin Mints in a list of the best selling cookies in the U.S. (behind Oreo and Chips Ahoy) despite being available only 3 months a year

25: percentage of Girl Scout cookie sales attributed to Thin Mints

COOKIES

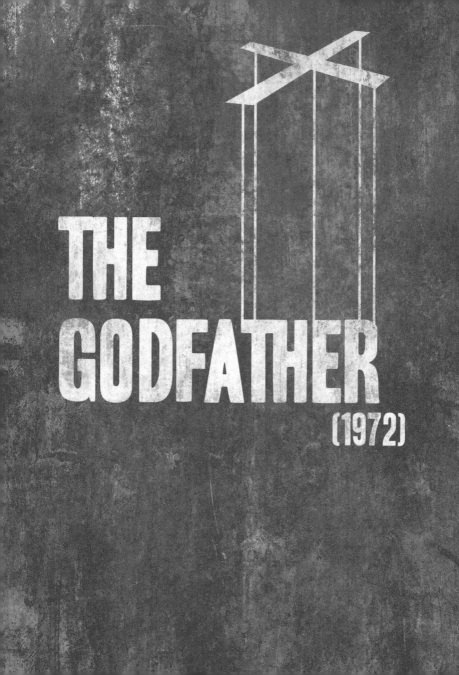

20: page count of the book outline on which Paramount based its decision to option *The Godfather*, even though Mario Puzo had yet to write the novel

4: actors Paramount executives wanted for the role of Vito Corleone (Ernest Borgnine, Edward G. Robinson, George C. Scott, and Orson Welles)

$100,000: fee for which Marlon Brando, who needed to resolve female-related money troubles, sold his "points" back to Paramount before the release of the film (a decision that would eventually cost him tens of millions of dollars)

200: "squibs" (fake blood pellets) used in Sonny's death scene at the Jersey Turnpike tollbooth, which was shot in one take

23: body count in *The Godfather,* including the horse

61: approximate number of scenes featuring food or people eating

0: times the terms "Mafia" and "Costa Nostra" are used in the script

GOLDEN GATE BRIDGE

1.7 miles: length of the Golden Gate Bridge

80,000 miles: length of wire that composes the two main cables of the Golden Gate Bridge

1,300: people who have jumped from the bridge since construction

219.3: section of the California Penal Code banning the scattering of a loved ones ashes off the bridge

173: the Pantone Matching System (PMS) code for the color ("International Orange") of the Golden Gate Bridge

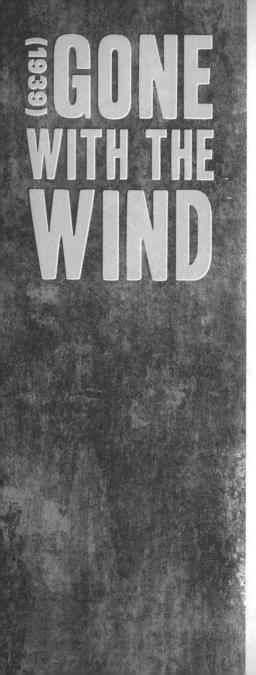

GONE WITH THE WIND (1939)

88 hours: length of film shot (standard industry average is 20 hours, for a 2-hour movie)

226 minutes: original running time of *Gone with the Wind*

20 minutes: running time of Doug Lothes one-man stage rendition of *Gone with the Wind*, in which he plays all the parts without sets or costumes

1,400: candidates interviewed for the part of Scarlett O'Hara

90: actresses given screen tests for the part of Scarlett O'Hara

1,100: horses used in the film

1,000: dummies used to augment the 1400 live extras hired for the Confederate Wounded Scene

8,000: times Elizabeth—a Brazilian woman who bought the pink percale dress worn by Scarlett (as Atlanta burned) at auction for $90,500—claims to have seen the movie

$1,542,500: price paid for the Best Picture Oscar awarded to producer David O. Selznick for *Gone with the Wind* in a 1999 auction at Sotheby's in New York (the winning bidder was Michael Jackson)

$0: amount producer David O. Selznick was fined by industry censors for using the word damn in Rhett Butler's famous exit line (it was allowed as it was taken directly from a literary work)

1: rank of "Frankly, my dear, I don't give a damn" in the American Film Institute's list of the 100 most memorable lines in cinema history

2,314: estimated number of live concerts the Grateful Dead played

145: numbers of concerts the Grateful Dead played in 1970, the most shows they ever played in one year

1: ranking most Deadheads would give the May 8, 1977 concert at Cornell University on a list of the Dead's best live shows (in recognition of the 30th anniversary of the show, the mayor of Ithaca, NY proclaimed May 8, 2007 "Grateful Dead Day")

1: Top 10 singles the Grateful Dead had in their career ("A Touch of Grey" in 1987)

.25 miles: distance that the "Wall of Sound," a 75-ton amplification system built for the Dead in the early 1970s, was capable of projecting quality playback

1 month: period following Jerry Garcia's death in 1995 where Ben & Jerry reportedly made Cherry Garcia ice cream using black cherries instead of Bing cherries as a show of mourning

$30 million: *Forbes* estimate of the Grateful Dead's current annual income

Harry

50,000: first printing for *Harry Potter and the Sorcerer's Stone*, the first in the series

8.3 million: copies sold of the seventh book in the series, *Harry Potter and the Deathly Hallows,* in the first 24 hours after publication

12 pounds: weight of *Deathly Hallows* Braille edition

62442: the secret code Arthur Weasley enters into the keypad when he takes Harry and his pals to the Ministry of Magic (the letters underneath those numbers on a standard telephone keypad spell out m-a-g-i-c)

159: page number in *Harry Potter and the Goblet of Fire*, where first-year student Natalie McDonald is assigned by the Sorting Hat to Gryffindor (the house for the brave at heart). McDonald was a 9-year-old

Potter

girl from Canada who had written Rowling wanting to know how the series turned out, as she was dying of leukemia; the author named the character in her honor

12: the maximum O.W.L.s (Ordinary Wizarding Levels) a witch or wizard can receive

3,000: approximate number of wizards in Britain

10: species of dragons

29: bronze knuts in a silver sickle, in wizard money (there are also 17 sickles in a gold galleon)

7: gold galleons it cost Harry to buy his magic wand

$10.25: approximate value of one gold galleon in U.S. dollars, based on 2008 exchange rates

2,500: estimated Hells Angels members in 230 chapters worldwide

20,000: miles a Hells Angel rides each year, on average

$500: value of the beer used as payment to the Hells Angels who provided security for the Rolling Stone's concert at Altamont Speedway (documented in the film *Gimme Shelter*) outside San Francisco in 1969

1%: symbol on one of the patches Hells Angels awards its members (derived from the comment made by the American Motorcyclist Association stating

that 99% of motorcyclists were law-abiding citizen, and the last 1% were outlaws)

81: symbol on the patches Hells Angels most commonly awards its members (the numbers stand for the respective position of the letters 'H' and 'A' in the alphabet)

$990,000: judgment awarded to Hells Angels following a botched raid of the club's property in 1998 by the Santa Clara County (California) police

2: trademark infringement lawsuits filed by Hells Angels, including one against the Walt Disney Company in 2006 alleging that the film *Wild Hogs* used both their name and distinctive logo without permission

ANGELS

HOLLYWOOD WALK OF FAME

3: animal actors who have been awarded stars on the Walk of Fame (Lassie, Rin Tin Tin, and Strongheart)

3.5 miles: length of the current Walk of Fame

5: number of industry categories (Motion Pictures, Television, Radio, Recording, and Live Theatre) in which a recipient can be honored

1: people who have received a star in every industry category for a total of 5 stars (Gene Autry)

4: stars that have been stolen and had to be replaced (Gregory Peck, James Stewart, Kirk Douglas, and Gene Autry)

18: age of Mary-Kate and Ashley Olson when they received their star in 2004, the youngest people to ever be awarded one

200: applications received each year for the approximately 24 stars selected

7: times (as of 2008) that Cheetah the Chimp (of *Tarzan* fame) has vied—unsuccessfully—to get a star

$25,000: amount paid in order for a recipient to be awarded a star (although this fee is commonly paid by a sponsor—such as a movie studio, television network, or record company—that stands to benefit from the resulting media attention)

(1951-1957)

I Love Lucy

23%: alcoholic content of Vitameatavegamin

3 inches: thickness of the extra padding that the prop department added to one side of the couch in the Ricardo living room, so Desi Arnaz, if seated, would look taller than he actually was

60 minutes: average time it took to film a half-hour *I Love Lucy* episode (the shortest filming time was 44 minutes), compared to the average 5 hours it takes to film a same-style sitcom today

71.8: percentage of the U.S. population who watched the birth of Little Ricky on January 19. 1953 (besting the 67.7% who watched the joint 3-network coverage of the inauguration of Dwight D. Eisenhower the next morning)

0: times the network censor allowed the word "pregnant" to be used on *I Love Lucy*

3: years Little Ricky aged over the summer of 1956 (hiatus between Seasons 5 and 6)

5 years, 7 months: difference in the real life ages of Lucille Ball and Desi Arnza (Lucy was older)

623: street number of the Ricardos' apartment building (on East 68th Street in New York City); in reality, the highest address on East 68th St, is 600, which means if the building actually existed, Lucy and Ricky's apartment would have been in the East River

JELL-O

1 million: packages of Jell-O that are purchased daily

40: percentage of Jell-O sold that is sugar free (first introduced in 1923, it was originally called D-Zerta)

1: fresh fruits that will not float in Jell-O (seedless grapes)

4: original flavors of Jell-O (strawberry, raspberry, lemon, and orange)

$7.95: price of a brain-shaped Jell-O mold from Seattle retailer Archie McPhee (trivia lovers take note: if Jell-O is hooked up to an EEG, it registers movements virtually identical to the brain waves of a healthy adult)

10 ounces: average amount of liquor (chilled) used to replace every 6 ounces of cold water (as called for in the directions on the box) in order to make Jell-O shots

14,000: number of signatures required—and gotten—to have Jell-O declared the "official State Snack of Utah" (there is more consumption of lime Jell-O in Salt Lake City than in anywhere else in the world)

30: number of years Bill Cosby was the commercial spokesperson for Jell-O

69: most points Michael Jordan scored in a single game (against Cleveland, March 28, 1990)

30.1: Michael Jordan's career average points per game (highest in NBA history)

5: times Michael Jordan was awarded NBA's Most Valuable Player

49: times Michael Jordan has been on the cover of *Sports Illustrated* (not only has he been on more covers than any other athlete, he has done so in four different uniforms and representing three different sports)

5 foot, 9 inches: maximum height of Michael Jordan's parents

12: Michael Jordan's jersey number, but only for one night (February 14, 1990) and only because an Orlando Magic Arena employee had stolen his #23 jersey

$5000: per game fine that the NBA (repeatedly) levied against Michael Jordan in 1985—for wearing Air Jordan I shoes when he played—claiming the shoes vibrant black-and-red color violated the league's uniform rules (a fine that p.r.-savvy Nike was more than happy to pay)

62: percentage of the purse guaranteed to the Derby's winner

$2,850: amount paid to Aristides, winner of the first Derby in 1875

$1,450,000: amount paid to Street Sense, winner of the Derby in 2007

1 minute, 59.40 seconds: time of Secretariat's win in 1973, the fastest in Derby history

KENTUCKY DERBY

554: red roses in the garland presented to the winner (hence the Derby's nickname, "Run for the Roses")

3: ingredients in a Mint Julep (bourbon, mint, simple syrup)

120,000: Mint Juleps served at Churchill Downs over the 2-day Derby weekend

$6,600: Stephen King's annual teacher's salary in 1973

$2,500: advance paid for *Carrie*, his first book, in 1973

$45 million: *Forbes* estimate of Stephen King's annual income in 2008

350 million: estimated number of Stephen King books that have been sold

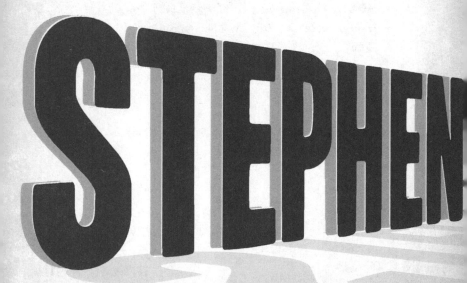

54: films produced that have been adapted from Stephen King's writings

5: adaptations of *Carrie* (the 1976 feature film, a 1988 Broadway musical, a 1999 feature film sequel, a 2002 television movie, and 2006 off-Broadway parody with a drag queen in the lead role)

217: room at the Overlook Hotel that chef Dick Hallorann warned five-year old Danny Torrance to avoid at all costs in *The Shining*

2: original colors of LEGO bricks (red and white)

55: current available colors of LEGO bricks

915,103,765: ways that six eight-stud LEGO bricks (of any color) can be combined

306 million: miniature rubber tires that the LEGO Group manufactures for their vehicles yearly (making them, ostensibly, the largest tire manufacturer in the world)

18: LEGO components out of every 1 million produced that have to be removed from a set because they fail to meet the company's quality control standards

1:20: scale replica of Miniland U.S.A., the recreation of famous American landmarks built out of over 20 million Lego bricks at LEGOLAND in Carlsbad, CA

3,600: dioramas, each made entirely out of LEGO bricks and elements, that California artist Brendan Powell Smith has built to retell 300 stories from the Bible

$60,000: price of a one-of-a-kind, life-size sculpture of you or a loved one by New York artist Nathan Sawaya, fashioned out of LEGO bricks

LORD OF THE RINGS

3 feet, 6 inches: average height of a hobbit

100 years: average lifespan of hobbits (adulthood begins at age 33)

$15,000: fee J.R.R. Tolkien was paid for the film rights in 1968

$2.91 billion: worldwide box office gross of the film trilogy

11: Academy Awards won by *The Return of the King* (which also tied the record held by *Ben-Hur* and *Titanic* for the most Oscars won by a single film)

8: actors, of the nine who portrayed the members of 'The Fellowship', who got a tattoo of the word 'nine' in Elvish to mark the close bond they built up during the eighteen months of filming the trilogy (Johyn Rhys-Davies was the lone hold-out)

1,600: pairs of latex hobbit feet made for the trilogy (there was no way of removing the feet at the end of the day without damaging them, so each pair could only be used once. Used feet were shredded to prevent a black market in stolen hobbit feet)

30: pounds Sean Astin gained for his role as Samwise

1,460: eggs served to the cast and crew every morning during filming

2,400: total crew members

1.6 million: downloads of the promotional trailer on April 7, 2001, within the first 24 hours that it was made available on the Internet

2: business partners (Forrest Mars and Bruce Murrie) who started a candy company in 1941 and combined their initials (M & M) to name their first product

400 million: M&Ms produced daily

12: percentage of M&Ms in a regular bag that are red (the most frequently found color is blue, at 22.2%)

11 years: time span (from 1976 to 1987) that red M&Ms were not available due to the FDA ban on red dye #2 (ironically, red M&Ms never contained the dye; they were only discontinued because company officials feared customers would THINK they did)

20: colors of M&Ms available on the Web for custom printing (the company prohibits customization that includes obscene text or initials that will make the candies look like medication)

126: article in the Van Halen contract that stated "There will be no brown M&M's in the backstage area, upon pain of forfeiture of the show, with full compensation." (in truth, the group cleverly requested this in order to have an easy way to identify that their contract had actually been read)

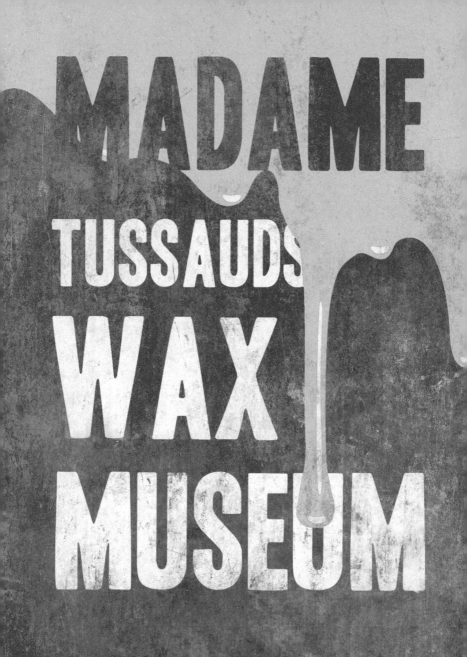

$150,000: minimum cost to make a Madame Tussauds wax figure

250: average number of photos Madame Tussauds needs to take of a celebrity in order to create a likeness

6 months: time it takes Madame Tussauds to make a wax figure from start to completion (5 weeks to complete the hair alone, since each piece is inserted in the head by hand)

1: celebrities who have turned down the invitation from Madam Tussauds to have a figure made in their likeness (Indian actor, director, and writer Aamir Kahn)

1: celebrities whose wax figure likeness appears in each of Madame Tussauds nine museums (Barack Obama)

5 minutes: time it took, after the Madame Tussauds museum in Berlin first opened its doors, for a protestor to tear off the head of the wax figure of Adolf Hitler

MADONNA

140: Madonna's reported IQ

16: consecutive singles, beginning with "Lucky Star" in 1984, that made the top five, a record for a female artist

7: number of weeks that "Take a Bow" was number one on the charts (although not considered one of Madonna's classics, it held that position longer than any of her other hit singles)

1: number of Madonna's singles that have failed to make the *Billboard* Top 100 ("Everybody" in 1982)

3 million: copies of Madonna's book *Sex* that were sold worldwide, making it the most successful coffee table book ever published

13: expletives uttered by Madonna during a 1994 interview with David Letterman

3,500: individual wardrobe items for Madonna's 2008–09 "Sticky & Sweet Tour"

5: number of people it takes to change Madonna's costumes during the "Sticky & Sweet Tour"

$40 million: amount Madonna earned in 2007

33 years: time span (1924–1957) that Marlboro was marketed as a woman's cigarette and featured a red tip so as to hide lipstick marks while smoking

.025: percentage of U.S. market-share Marlboro had before the introduction of the Marlboro Man advertising campaign in 1957

40.8: percentage of U.S. market share Marlboro had as of 2007

2: actors, of the 14 who have portrayed the Marlboro man, who have died of lung cancer (a third died of emphysema)

1: rank of the Marlboro Man in the list of "The 101 Most Influential People Who Never Lived"

MCDONALD'S

40: percentage of company profits that are attributed to the sales of happy meals

$2,250: cost to purchase 100 shares of McDonald's stock when the company went public in 1965

$3.3 million: value of that stock (which would have multiplied into 74,360 shares) as of 2007

58 million: customers McDonald's serves in a single day (at 31,000 restaurants in 119 countries)

700: seating capacity of the largest McDonald's (Beijing, China)

1 out of 8: percentage of people in the U.S. who have worked at McDonald's

23,000: minimum number of Big Macs consumed by Don Gorske of Fond du Lac, WI since May 17, 1972 (he eats at least two a day)

24.5 lbs.: weight gain experienced by Morgan Spurlock during the 30-day period in 2004 when he ate nothing but McDonald's meals for the documentary *Super Size Me*

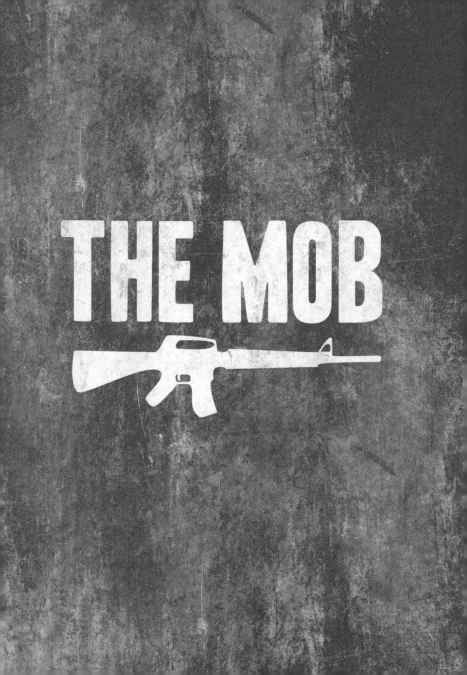

$127 billion: money in the Italian economy generated annually by organized crime

$43 billion: money organized crime takes in annually just from interest on loans

7: percentage of Italy's gross domestic product accounted for by organized crime

80: estimated percentage of the businesses in the Sicilian cities of Catania and Palermo that regularly pay the Mob *pizzo* (protection money)

5: Italian-American families that have dominated organized crime in New York City since the 1930s (Bonanno, Gambino, Colombo, Genovese, and Luchesse)

2: rank of "Never look at the wives of friends" in the list of ten 'commandments' that bind the members of the Mob

27: actors who appeared in *Goodfellas* who also appeared in *The Sopranos*

MONOPOLY

52: the "number of fundamental playing errors" cited by Parker Bros. in their evaluation of the Monopoly game (and the reason it was unanimously rejected when Charles Darrow submitted it to them in 1934)

$15,140: total amount of money in a standard Monopoly game

27: languages in which the Monopoly game is published (including Croatian and Icelandic)

22: properties on the Monopoly game board that can be built upon

1: properties on the Monopoly game board not named after a street (Marvin Gardens— which is an Atlantic City neighborhood—and which, had it been spelled correctly, should have been Marven Gardens)

6: metal tokens in the original 1935 Monopoly game (iron, cannon, thimble, ship, shoe, and top hat)

20: percentage of Monopoly players who prefer the racecar token over the eleven others currently offered

$25,000: the cost of the Monopoly game made by Alfred Dunhill, which included gold hotels and silver houses

1,680 hours: length of the longest game of Monopoly ever played (lasting over 70 days)

Marilyn Monroe

$5: payment Marilyn Monroe received for first modeling job

$500: amount Hugh Hefner paid in 1952 to gain the rights to Tom Kelley's nude photo of Marilyn Monroe

9: shades of blonde Marilyn Monroe tried before deciding on platinum

15: times a day Marilyn Monroe washed her face for fear of blemishes

5: toes on Marilyn Monroe's left foot (the rumor she had six is attributed to a photo taken on a beach in 1946 where the sand made it appear as if she had an extra toe)

40: takes it took before Marilyn Monroe finally got the classic subway scene in *The Seven Year Itch* right

20: works by Andy Warhol that included an image of Marilyn Monroe

600: books written about Marilyn Monroe (including 300 biographies)

Marilyn Monroe
(continued)

24: crypt number in Corridor of Memories at Westwood Cemetery in Los Angeles where Marilyn Monroe is buried

2: Number of times per week that ex-husband Joe DiMaggio had roses delivered to Marilyn Monroe's burial site for 20 years

$1,267,500: price paid (at a Christie's auction in 1999) for the "JFK Gown" Marilyn Monroe wore when she sang "Happy Birthday, Mr. President" (the sale set the record for the highest price ever paid for a single article of clothing)

$1.6 million: value of Monroe's estate on her death in 1962

$6.5 million: income derived from sales of Marilyn Monroe licensed products in 2008

$100,000: amount actress Veronica Hamel and her husband spent to remove the sophisticated bugging device (standard FBI issue and not commercially available) that they discovered in Marilyn Monroe's home when they bought (and remodeled) it in 1972

75%: Motown's "hit ratio" (percentage of the records they released that made the national charts)

3: versions of "I Heard It through the Grapevine" that were recorded by Motown artists (the Miracles, the Isley Brothers, and Gladys Knight & the Pips) before Marvin Gaye released his version, which topped the singles charts for 7 weeks

9 weeks: longest period of time a Motown single has stayed at number one on the U.S. charts ("Endless Love" by Diana Ross & Lionel Richie)

4.2 million: copies sold in the U.S. of the Jackson Five's "I'll Be There", making it Motown's best-selling single

22: Grammys won by Motown's Stevie Wonder, a record for a solo artist

22: men who have sung with the Temptations

MOUNT RUSHMORE

14 years: time it took to finish the project, with Gutzon Borglum, the sculptor who created it, dying seven months before completion

10,000 years: time it will take for Mount Rushmore (which is made of a durable, fine-grained granite) to erode just one inch

400: workers involved in the construction of Mount Rushmore

506: steps workers had to climb every day to the construction site

0: deaths during construction

465 feet: how tall a man scaled to the size of the carvings would stand

700 lbs.: weight of the brick of cheddar used by carver Troy Landwehr to recreate Mount Rushmore out of cheese

100: number of DVDs of Alfred Hitchcock's *North by Northwest* sold yearly in the Mount Rushmore gift shop—ironic, considering the National Park Service tried to stop the movie, which they felt desecrated the memorial with scenes of violence

NASCAR

293 feet: distance that a NASCAR driver, going the standard 200 mph on a straight-away, travels in one second

100 degrees: average temperature of the interior of the car during a NASCAR race (with temperatures rising as high as 170 degrees by the floorboards)

10: pounds of sweat a NACAR driver can lose during a race

3: Gs of force a NASCAR driver can experience against their bodies while making a turn, comparable to the forces pressing down on shuttle astronauts at liftoff

128: Gs of force experienced by Jerry Nadeau at Richmond International Speedway in 2003, the hardest NASCAR crash on record

120 to 150: heart rate (in beats per minute) that a NASCAR driver maintains throughout a standard 3-hour race (about the same as a serious marathon runner)

National

33 MINUTES: AVERAGE TIME THAT A PERSON WHO BUYS THE *ENQUIRER* SPENDS READING IT

93: percentage of *Enquirer* readers that suffer from diabetes (as compared to 44% of the readers of other entertainment weeklies such as *People, Us,* or *In Touch*)

4: PERCENTAGE OF *ENQUIRER* READERS WHO BELIEVE ALL OR MOST OF WHAT THE PAPER PUBLISHES

Enquirer

61: PERCENTAGE OF *ENQUIRER* READERS WHO BELIEVE NOTHING OF WHAT THE PAPER PUBLISHES

27: number of years the *Enquirer* went without being successfully sued

$750,000: amount paid by the *Enquirer* in punitive damages to Carol Burnett in 1981 after publishing a fabricated story that she had been spotted drunk at a restaurant where Henry Kissinger was in attendance

2.8 miles: average length of a New York City cab ride

30: average number of fares a New York City taxi driver picks up in a 12-hour shift

60: languages spoken by New York City taxi drivers

85: nationalities of New York City taxi drivers

$25: amount a licensed taxi driver can be fined, according to the civil code of New York City, for wearing shorts on the job

$750,000: price (as of 2009) of the official medallion issued by the Taxi and Limousine Commission that authorizes a corporation to legally operate a yellow cab in New York City

22 million: gallons of gas expected to be saved each year, starting in 2012, when all of New York City's 13,000 licensed taxi cabs will be hybrids

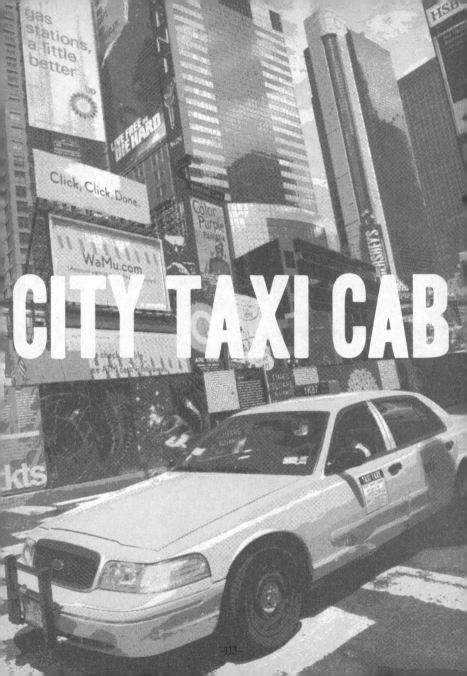

CITY TAXI CAB

The New

1,612: page count of the largest edition of *The New York Times* ever published (it was delivered on September 14, 1987 and weighed 12 pounds)

138,000: words of news published in an average edition of *The New York Times*

9: number of corrections *The New York Times* averages daily

York Times

225: squares in *The New York Times* crossword puzzle, which increases in difficulty from Monday to Saturday (the Sunday puzzle is as difficult as the Thursday puzzle, but it is larger and contains 441 squares)

10,000: bookstores and retailers whose sales are used to determine which titles make *The New York Times* best seller list

98: PULITZER PRIZES WON BY THE NEW YORK TIMES

NIAGARA FALLS

150,000 gallons: volume of water that flows over the U.S. side of Niagara Falls every second

170 feet: depth of the Niagara River, just below the Falls

63: age of the first person (a female dance teacher) to go over Niagara Falls in a barrel and survive

$100: price of a marriage license from the city of Niagara Falls

50,000: honeymooners who visit Niagara Falls each year ("The Honeymoon Capital of the World")

2 to 1: ratio of visitors to the Canadian side of Niagara Falls to those who visit on the U.S. side (thanks to better views and more dramatic falls)

THE OPRAH

141: countries, from Australia to Zimbabwe, that broadcast *The Oprah Winfrey Show*

20: seasons *The Oprah Winfrey Show* has been the number one-rated daytime talk show on television

300: size of the audience at a taping of *The Oprah Winfrey Show*

19 to 1: ratio of women to men in the studio audience of *The Oprah Winfrey Show*

856: celebrities who have been guests on *The Oprah Winfrey Show*

12: times Julia Roberts has appeared on *The Oprah Winfrey Show*, more than any other celebrity

WINFREY SHOW

(1986-)

90 million: viewers who tuned in to watch the interview with Michael Jackson on February 10, 1993, the highest rated episode (39.3 rating/56 share) in the history of *The Oprah Winfrey Show*

2 million: approximate number of online members in Oprah's Book Club

$70 million: money that has been raised to date (2009) through Oprah's Angel Network (among the results: 55 schools built in 12 countries)

$7,000: average amount in taxes that each of the 276 audience members of *The Oprah Winfrey Show* who received a new Pontiac G6 in September 2004, had to pay on the gift

THE OSCAR

$500: cost to make an Oscar statue (compared to $100 for the Pulitzer Prize)

93: percentage of the Oscar statue that is made of tin (although the gold gilded over the metal statue is 24-karat)

8.5 lbs.: weight of an Oscar statue

5,900: approximate membership of the Academy of Arts and Sciences (and hence, the approximate number of Oscar voters)

40 minutes: minimum time a feature film can run in order for it to be eligible for a "Best Picture" Oscar nomination

59: Oscar nominations for Walt Disney, the most of any individual

4: Oscars won by Katherine Hepburn, the most of any actor

3: people who have won an Oscar and refused it (George C. Scott, Marlon Brando, and screenwriter Dudley Nichols)

55: Oscar statues that were stolen in route to the Awards in 2000 (2 are still missing)

94%: brand recognition of Pac-Man with American consumers (the highest of any video game character)

350,000: units of Pac-Man sold, making it the best-selling arcade game of all time

3,333,360: maximum possible score for a single game of Pac-Man, if a player completes all 255 levels, eats every pellet, fruit, and ghost—and does it all without dying once

4: number of ghosts (Blinky, Pinky, Inky, and Clyde) that can cause Pac-Man to lose a life

6 hours: approximate time it takes to play a perfect game of Pac Man

10: players needed for PacManhattan, a life-size, real-world version of the game that uses the streets around Washington Square Park in New York City as the grid

17,897: daily and Sunday *Peanuts* strips that Charles Schulz produced

2,600: newspapers which ran *Peanuts* during its peak popularity, providing a readership of 355 million in 75 countries (and making Charles Schulz the most visible artist in the world)

20,000: Peanuts-related products that have been licensed and created, included 1,400 book titles

20: percentage of Hallmark cards sold that feature a *Peanuts* character

$.05: price of Lucy's psychiatric advice ("The doctor is in")

0: times Charlie Brown successfully kicked the football while Lucy was holding it

10: football games that Charlie Brown's team won in the strip's 50-year history (number of games Charlie Brown didn't play in: the same 10)

842: estimated different character "heads" that have topped Pez dispensers since they were first introduced in 1954

4: real people, not fictional characters, whose likenesses have been reproduced as Pez "heads" (Betsy Ross, Daniel Boone, Paul Revere, and three versions of Elvis)

30 to 40: number of different Pez designs on the market at any given time

13: flavors of Pez candies currently offered (some of the more unusual that have appeared— and then disappeared—include anise, licorice, eucalyptus, yogurt and chlorophyll)

6: annual Pez conventions held in the U.S. (California, Connecticut, Minnesota, Missouri, Ohio, South Carolina)

$11,211.11: highest authenticated price paid for a Pez dispenser, a vintage transparent 1950s Space Gun sold on eBay in December, 2005

3 million: copies of *Playboy* currently sold monthly (half of what it was in the early 1970s, but still, the largest selling men's magazine in the world)

$25,000: current fee for a centerfold photo shoot

11: times Pamela Anderson has appeared on the cover of *Playboy*, more than any other person

140 lbs: heaviest weight of a Playmate (Anna Nicole Smith in 1992; average weight is 115 pounds)

5: rank of "the beach" in the list of top five Playmate "turn-ons" (after music, animals, eating, and clothes)

55: age of actress Terry Moore when she appeared nude in a (1984) *Playboy* pictorial, the oldest woman to do so

$8000: possible value of the first issue of *Playboy*, in mint condition

21,987: square footage of the Playboy Mansion in Los Angeles

1: current locations of the Playboy Club (Las Vegas)

Play-Doh

1: original colors of Play-Doh (off-white)

13: ingredients in Play-Doh (Play-Doh's exact composition is a trade secret, but the patent indicates it contains the following: water, a starch-based binder, a retrogradation inhibitor, salt, lubricant, surfactant, preservative, hardener, humectant, fragrance, and color. A petroleum additive gives the compound a smooth feel, and borax prevents mold from developing)

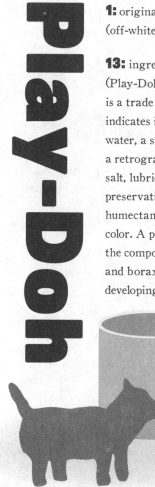

22 years: how long the Play-Doh formula was used to make wallpaper cleaner before the company who manufactured it realized it could also be marketed and sold to schools as a pliable modeling clay

$.34: price Kutol Products charged for a can of their wallpaper cleaner in 1955

$1.50: price Rainbow Crafts (a subsidiary of Kutol Products) charged for the same size container of Play-Doh in 1955

2000: miniature Play-Doh bricks, molded by hand, that a Charlottesville, Virginia architectural firm used to build a scale replica model of Monticello

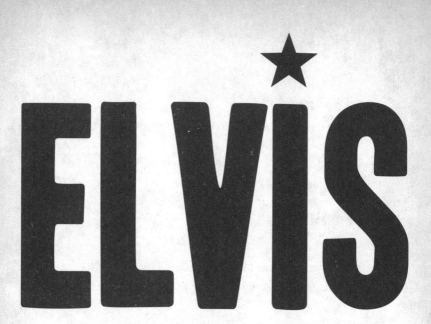

1 billion: Elvis record units sold worldwide to date, more than any other musical artist

104: Elvis songs to make the Top 40 on the *Billboard* 100, more than any other musical artist

500: members of the Professional Elvis Impersonators Association

$102,000: price Elvis paid for Graceland in 1957

PRESLEY

$300,000: price paid for Elvis' favorite performance costume, the peacock jumpsuit, sold in an online auction by Gotta Have It in 2008

53310761: serial number of U.S. Army private Presley, inducted in 1958

31: number of feature films Elvis made

625: Elvis fan clubs worldwide

ELVIS PRESLEY

(continued)

4: rank of the black-and-white picture of Elvis meeting Richard Nixon in 1970 on the list of the "most requested photographs" in the holdings of the National Archives and Records Administration in Washington, D.C. (1–3 are images of Pearl Harbor, D-Day, and Hiroshima)

6.5 million: copies of the *National Enquirer* sold the week of Elvis Presley's death in 1977, after Elvis's distant cousin sold a photo of him in a coffin to the *Enquirer* for $18,000

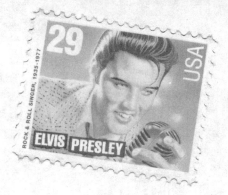

500 million: Elvis stamps printed by the United States Postal Service in 1993, three times the usual print run for a commemorative stamp (the Elvis stamp remains the top selling commemorative postage stamp of all time)

$52 million: amount Elvis' estate earned in 2008, 30 years after his death, making him #1 on "Top Earning Dead Celebrities" list in *Forbes* magazine

$9,000: price Alfred Hitchcock paid to anonymously option Robert Bloch's novel (he then bought up as many copies of the book as possible so he could keep the ending a secret)

70: DIFFERENT CAMERA ANGLES IN THE 45-SECOND SHOWER SCENE IN *PSYCHO*

7 days: time it took to shoot the shower scene

(1960)
PSYCHO

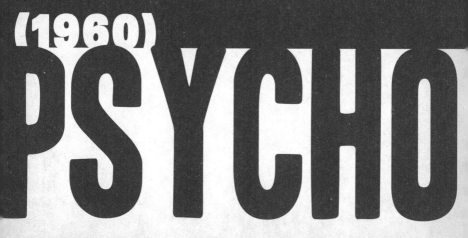

$40,000: FEE ANTHONY PERKINS WAS PAID, THE EXACT AMOUNT THAT THE CHARACTER MARION CRANE EMBEZZLED IN THE FILM

$250,000: salary Alfred Hitchcock deferred when he opted to take 60% of the films net profits (ultimately he would earn more more than $15 million)

15,000: phone calls QVC typically receives per hour

1,150: products presented on QVC each week

25: percentage of the products presented each week that are new to the QVC customer

364: days a years that QVC broadcasts live, 24 hours a day (the only day of the year that programming is pre-recorded is Christmas)

3,000: applications QVC receives per year for host positions (the typical hire is 3)

$112 million: QVC's revenues for its first fiscal year (while a record for sales of a new public company, current annual net sales top $7.4 billion)

$80 million: highest QVC sales day ever, on December 2, 2001 (the most popular item offered was the Dell Intel Pentium IV personal computer)

43,000: copies of Barry Manilow's CD *The Greatest Songs of the Sixties* that were ordered in one hour on October 21, 2006 (a network record for music sales)

400,000: Supersmile Whitening Systems that have been sold on QVC to date, making it one of the network's top selling items ever

RADIO CITY
ROCKETTES

———————⭐———————

5 feet, 6 inches: minimum height requirement to be a Rockette

5 feet, 10 1/2 inches: maximum height allowable to be a Rockette

36: Rockettes comprising the dance line

200: "eye-high" kicks performed each show

9: costume changes per show

1 million: number of people who see the Rockettes in the annual Radio City Christmas Spectacular

27: number of individual cubes that make up one Rubik's Cube

43 quintillion: combinations to solve the 3x3x3 Rubik's Cube

1 month: time it took Ernö Rubik, the Hungarian inventor of the cube, to solve his puzzle

22: the least amount of twists needed to solve the Rubik's Cube

325: number of books written about how to solve the Rubik's cube

38,000: videos on YouTube, mainly tutorials, that feature the Rubik's Cube

7.08 seconds: current (2009) world record for solving the 3x3x3 Rubik's Cube, held by Erik Akkersdijk of the Netherlands

RUBIK'S
CUBE

4,000: estimated number of animals (of more than 800 species) that roam the San Diego Zoo

6: maximum capacity of the Giant Panda Research Station (currently the facility houses Giant Pandas)

40: types of bamboo the San Diego Zoo grows to feed the pandas (they also grow 18 types of eucalyptus to feed the Koalas)

2,500: ginger plants that provide the fragrance for Sun Bear Forest

40 degrees: regulated temperature on the chartered cargo plane used to fly a herd of seven

SAN DIEGO

African elephants from Swaziland to San Diego
in 2003 after they were scheduled to be culled for
overpopulation

7: New Guinea Singing Dogs at the San Diego Zoo
(the largest number found in one place in the world)

1 in 10,000: occurrence rate of a two-headed snake
such as the one (Thelma and Louise) that lived at the
San Diego Zoo in the 1990s

66: appearances that Joan Embery, Goodwill
Ambassador to the San Diego Zoo, made on *The
Tonight Show* with Johnny Carson

5 days: time span between the song title and guitar riff coming to Keith Richards in a dream and "Satisfaction" being recorded (it would then be only three weeks before it was released)

10 minutes: time it took Mick Jagger to write the lyrics to "Satisfaction" the morning after Richards's dream

4 weeks: how long "Satisfaction" was number one on the *Billboard* Hot 100 (it was the first number one hit for the Rolling Stones in the U.S.)

2: rank of "Satisfaction" on *Rolling Stone* magazine's list of the 500 Great Songs of All Time (Bob Dylan's "Like a Rolling Stone" is their number one)

45: the age Mick Jagger referenced when he said he "would rather be dead than be singing 'Satisfaction'" (oops!)

"(I Can't Get No) SATISFACTION"

SATs

1520: average score on the SAT (out of a possible 2400)

1206: George W. Bush's SAT score, when the highest possible score was 1600 (Bill Clinton received a 1032)

1: possible answers that anyone taking the SAT needs to be able to eliminate in a multiple choice question in order to make it statistically better to guess the answer than leave it blank

0: number of analogy questions on the current SAT (analogy questions, which once made up one quarter of the questions in the Verbal section of the SAT, were eliminated when the test was revamped in 2005)

775: four-year colleges that do not require the SAT

4,400: students (out of the 495,000) who took the SAT in October 2006 whose tests were incorrectly scored because the pages got damp and did not scan properly (a class action suit was filed and settled for $2.85 million)

100%: how much of Nik Cohn's 1976 *New York* magazine cover story "Tribal Rites of the New Saturday Night" (which he claimed was based on extensive interviews and research)—and on which *Saturday Night Fever* was based—was completely fabricated

$2,000: price film critic Gene Siskel paid for the iconic white disco suit John Travolta wore in *Saturday Night Fever* (he outbid Jane Fonda for it; her best offer was $1,900)

$145,000: price film critic Gene Siskel sold the iconic white disco suit for in 1995, eighteen years later

20 lbs: weight that John Travolta lost while making *Saturday Night Fever*, mainly from dancing 3 hours a day

40 lbs: weight that Donna Pescow put on for her role as Annette

24: weeks the *Saturday Night Fever* sound track (which would eventually go platinum 17 times) held the number one spot on the *Billboard* albums chart

120,000: possible words, according to the National Scrabble Association, that can be spelled out using seven letters or fewer

101: possible 2-letter words, from "aa" to "za," that are acceptable to use in Scrabble

200: official Scrabble clubs in the U.S.

170: official Scrabble championships

$25,000: prize for the National Scrabble
Championship

128 points: highest possible opening score in
a game of Scrabble (achievable by using the word
"muzjiks", meaning "Russian peasants")

830 points:

highest individual
score on record
for a single game
of Scrabble (by
Michael Cresta, a
carpenter from
Massachusetts, on
October 12, 2006)

365 points:

highest single play
in a game of Scrabble, again by Michael Cresta (for
using "quixotry")

61: squares on the Scrabble board, out of 225 total,
worth extra points

SESAME STREET

(1969-)

8 million: American children who watch *Sesame Street* every week

180: countries where *Sesame Street* has aired

210: times the letter "B" has sponsored the show

95: percentage of American preschoolers who have watched Sesame Street

8 feet, 2 inches: height of Big Bird

4,000: approximate number of feathers in Big Bird's costume (which, for the record, are actually turkey feathers, died yellow)

368: bottle caps in Bert's collection

65 (triple G): shoes size of Snuffleupagus

871: number of the episode where Mr. Hooper got his diploma—and where it was revealed that his first name was "Harold"

341: celebrities who have "visited" *Sesame Street* through 2008 (James Earl Jones was the first)

$1,500: highest price paid for a $28.99 Tickle-Me Elmo doll in 1996 when unexpected demand resulted in short supply

117: Emmys won by *Sesame Street* as of 2008 (more than any other television program)

Dr. Seuss

(Theodore Geisel)

27: times Dr. Seuss's first book, *And to Think That I Saw It on Mulberry Street*, was rejected before being published by Vanguard Press

225: number of standard "new-reader" words on the vocabulary list from which Dr. Seuss wrote *The Cat in the Hat*

$50: amount Dr. Seuss's editor (Bennett Cerf) bet Dr. Seuss that he could not write a book using fewer than 50 different words (Cerf lost; Seuss wrote *Green Eggs and Ham*)

4: rank of *Green Eggs and Ham* on *Publisher Weekly's* list of the bestselling children's books of all time

$4,000: current market-value price of a first edition copy of *The Cat in the Hat*

53: years the Grinch wished to keep Christmas from coming in *How the Grinch Stole Christmas*

2: size difference between the Grinch's heart and a normal heart (the Grinch's was "two sizes too small")

13: books Dr. Seuss wrote under the name Theo. LeSieg ("LeSieg" is "Geisel" spelled backwards; Geisel used this second pseudonym on any book that he wrote, but did not illustrate)

THE SIMPSONS

(1989-)

48: series of two-minute animated shorts that ran on the *The Tracey Ullman Show* from 1987–1989, featuring the members of a dysfunctional family before the characters were spun off into their own half-hour prime time show named *The Simpsons*

9: spikes of hair on Bart's head

10: eternal age of Bart on the show

2 years, 38 days: how much older Bart is than Lisa

6 to 8 months: approximate time it takes to produce a half-hour episode of *The Simpsons*, from start to finish

160: minimum numbers of characters Hank Azaria (best-known as the voice of Moe the bartender, Apu the Kwik-E-Mart owner, and Police Chief Wiggum) has voiced on the series (more than any other actor)

$847.63: the price of Maggie in the original opening sequence (the figure was, at the time *The Simpsons* premiered, the standard amount of money required to raise a baby for one month in the U.S.)

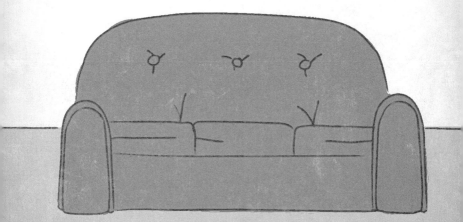

FRANK SINATRA

40: song recordings (including "I'll Never Smile Again") that Sinatra released in his first year (1940) with the Tommy Dorsey Band

30,000: Sinatra fans who caused a near riot outside the Paramount Theatre in New York before his October 11, 1944 show, when they were unable to get in

58: movies Sinatra appeared in (he won the supporting actor Oscar for *From Here to Eternity* in 1953)

0: times Sinatra referred to himself and his group of Hollywood friends as "The Rat Pack" ("The Rat Pack" was a term used by journalists and outsiders; to Sinatra, they were "the Summit" or "the Clan")

4 hours: how long it took Paul Anka to write "My Way" for Sinatra in 1969, after Sinatra told him over dinner that he was quitting the record business

3 hours: average time it took Sinatra to record an album

1 billion: kilowatt dam Sinatra sang about in "High Hopes"

1,275: pages in Frank Sinatra's FBI files, which were released to the public after his death

86: coil turns in a standard metal Slinky

63: feet of wire in a standard metal Slinky

11 seconds: maximum time it takes for specially engineered machines to manufacture a Slinky (the toy only looks simple; the process is so intricate that in the 1970s when Xerox had trouble producing a coiled spring that they needed for a copier, they had the work done at the Slinky factory)

23 years: length of time the Slinky song (*It's Slinky, it's Slinky/for fun it's a won-der-ful toy/ It's Slinky, it's Slinky/it's fun for a girl and a boy*) was continuously used in the company's television commercials, making it the longest-running jingle in advertising history

1340: approximate page number in Webster's *New World Dictionary* (College Edition) where the word "slinky" is found (and the same place where, in 1943, Betty James found the perfect name for the "toy" her husband Richard invented)

Snow White and the Seven Dwarfs (1937)

15: age that Walt Disney first imagined an animated version of the story of Snow White after seeing a silent film adaptation in 1917

50: names on the list from which the names for the Seven Dwarfs were chosen (among those considered and later rejected were Awful, Blabby, Hotsy and Shifty)

8: songs used in the film (out of the 25 that were written specifically for it)

2 million: illustrations created for the film (using 1,500 shades of paint)

$5: bonus that Walt Disney would pay an animator for coming up with a sight gag that ultimately was used in the movie

2: cartoon paintings of Bashful and Doc, inspired by the movie, recently found by a war museum in Norway that are believed to be the work of Adolf Hitler (Hitler tried to make a living as an artist before his rise to power)

$100: money paid to Kenneth Daigneau (a New York actor and brother of a Hormel V.P.) in 1937 for being the one to come up with the name SPAM (a contraction of "spiced ham")

6: ingredients in SPAM (ham, pork, sugar, salt, water and a little potato starch, which is what both holds the shape and gives the meat a "lightness")

3.8: cans of SPAM consumed every second in America (Hawaiians eat more than anyone else—about 4 cans per person per year)

14%: increase in sales of SPAM beginning April 2008, a result of the economic crisis and the rising cost of food

$3,000: prize money currently awarded to the winning recipe in the annual Great American SPAM Championships held at state fairs throughout the country

19,696: haikus that have been written devoted to SPAM

16,500 square feet: size of the SPAM Museum in Austin, MN

$65: cost of a life-size SPAM can costume carried in the gift shop at the SPAM museum (or in the SPAM store online)

87,000: possible drink combinations available at Starbucks, once you factor in shots, syrups, choice of whipped/not whipped, etc.

35 million: people who visit a Starbucks store each week

4.4 million: total CDs sold in Starbucks stores each year

241%: increase in sales of jazz singer Madeleine Peyroux's album *Careless Love* after just one week of being available in Starbucks stores

$114 million: amount Starbucks was sued by a New York City customer after the company cancelled a "free coffee" email coupon within 24-hours of distributing it (the figure was equal to the cost of drinks for all those who were turned away once the offer was retracted)

630: calories in Venti White Chocolate Blended Creme Frappuccino, without whipped cream, more than any other drink on Starbucks' menu

STAR

16: productions that have been spun off from the original *Star Trek*, including 5 television series (4 live-action and 1 animated) and 11 feature films (together, the largest number of entities derived from a pre-existing show in TV history)

79: episodes (of the 79 in the series) that featured Leonard Nimoy as Captain Spock (the only character to appear in every episode of *Star Trek*)

TREK

52: the highest *Star Trek* ever ranked in the Nielsen ratings (out of approximately 80 primetime programs) although it was number one with viewers ages 16 to 39, which is why it lasted the three seasons that it did

230: chapters of the International Star Trek Fan Association

18: annual Star Trek conventions held worldwide

STAR TREK continued

40: video games with 'Star Trek' in the title

4: fingers on Scotty's right hand (James Dooahn, the actor who played Scotty, had lost his middle finger during World War II and most of his scenes were shot to hide it)

11 feet: size of the studio model of the USS *Enterprise* (which is now on display in the National Air and Space Museum of the Smithsonian Institution in Washington, D.C.)

8: standard warp speed of the USS *Enterprise*

$265,000: price paid for Captain Kirk's command chair and platform from the Bridge set of the USS *Enterprise*, in an auction on June 27, 2002 in Los Angeles (making it the most expensive piece of *Star Trek* memorabilia ever sold)

0: times Captain Kirk actually said "Beam me up, Scotty"

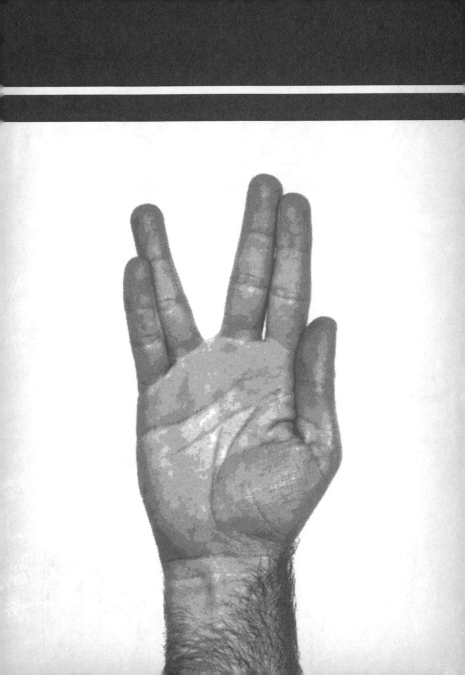

STAR WARS (1977)

40%: share of the *Star Wars* merchandising rights 20th Century Fox willingly handed over to George Lucas in lieu of a larger salary, because the studio felt they would be worthless

10 seconds: length of time it took George Lucas after first meeting Peter Mayhew to cast him as Chewbacca (all the 7'2" Mayhew had to do was stand up)

1138: cell block on the *Death Star* from which Luke claimed to be transferring Chewbacca, although there is an homage to the number 1138 (either in dialogue or in the set design) in all six episodes of the *Star Wars* franchise (the reason? *THX 1138* was George Lucas's first film)

6: times the *Star Wars* franchise has been featured on the cover of *Time* magazine

40: theaters that originally agreed to show *Star Wars* (the low interest prompted Fox to threaten that any theater that refused to run the film would not be given the rights to screen the eagerly anticipated *The Other Side of Midnight*—which, in the end, grossed less than 10% of what *Star Wars* did)

2.5: percentage of *Star Wars* profits that George Lucas (still) pays to Stephen Spielberg, a result of Lucas's wager that Spielberg's *Close Encounters* would beat his film at the box office (Spielberg bet it wouldn't—and it didn't)

10 lbs.: weight Carrie Fisher was required to lose before filming

18: different ways of breathing that were tried before Lucas found the mechanical sound he liked for Darth Vader

1: rank of the *Star Wars* film score in the American Film Institute's list of the Top 25 Film Scores of All Time

STATUE OF LIBERTY

354: steps to the top of the Statue of Liberty

305 feet, 1 inch: height of the Statue of Liberty from the ground to the tip of the flame

4 feet, 6 inches: length of the Statue of Liberty's nose

879: shoe size of the Statue of Liberty, based on the standard formula

7: spikes in the Statue of Liberty's crown (the seven spikes represent the seven seas and seven continents of the world)

3 inches: how much the Statue of Liberty sways in 50 m.p.h. winds

3: Statues of Liberty that currently stand in Paris (the scale model from which the original was fabricated, the replica in Luxembourg Gardens, and the one that is a gift to France from the community of Americans living in Paris)

570 million: estimated copies of Danielle Steel books in print

0: number of Danielle Steel's books that have not been a bestseller

390 weeks: consecutive period of time that Danielle Steel had at least one novel on *The New York Times* bestseller list

5: number of books Steel reportedly works on simultaneously (she might be researching one storyline, writing another, and editing a third)

22: Danielle Steel books that have been adapted for television

MARTHA

1: rank of "Macaroni and Cheese" in the list of most-requested recipes (of the thousands of recipes) *Martha Stewart Living* has published to date

4 hours: average amount of sleep Martha Stewart requires nightly (a self-professed insomniac, she watches lots of late-night and cable-access television, which is how she discovered her pet expert, Marc Morrone)

$1.49: suggested retail price of the felt-tipped Le Pen, Martha Stewart's favorite (depending on what she is signing, she uses black, brown, or blue; however, she always turns to red for the holidays)

STEWART

96%: Martha Stewart's control of voting power in MSLO

$230,000: value of ImClone stock Martha Stewart sold and lied about to investigators in 2004 (she later paid MSLO stockholders $30,000,000 for losses suffered during the scandal)

10 pounds: weight Martha lost while serving 5 months in jail (the only food she liked were chicken wings from the vending machine)

72: footballs that the NFL has manufactured annually, exclusively for use in the Super Bowl

$10 billion: value of Super Bowl bets that are placed annually

SUPER BOWL

$4,300: average price to buy a ticket to the Super Bowl through an agent or scalper (as opposed to the $700 to $900 face value)

$25,000: value of the Tiffany-made Vince Lombardi Trophy, given to the winner of the Super Bowl

$5,000: value of a Super Bowl ring, which is given to approximately 150 people

1,300: average calories consumed by one person at a typical Super Bowl party through food alone (factor in beer, soda or wine and the calories count can climb as high as 2,500)

20%: increase in sales of antacids the Monday after the Super Bowl

1.5 million: people who call in sick (real or not) the Monday after the Super Bowl

6 million: people who visit YouTube in the 48 hours following the Super Bowl to watch the commercials that aired during it

TIFFANY & CO.

0: number of jewelry items sold at Tiffany & Co. on opening day in September, 1837 (it began as Tiffany, Young and Ellis, a stationary store)

$4.98: total sales on Tiffany & Co.'s opening day

90: percentage of alleged Tiffany & Co. goods found on eBay that the company claims to be counterfeit

$807,000: price paid for the little black dress worn by Audrey Hepburn in the opening scenes of

Breakfast at Tiffany's in a December 4, 2006 auction at Christie's in London, making it the second most expensive piece of movie memorabilia ever sold

2: times that "Tiffany's" is mentioned in the song *Diamonds Are a Girl's Best Friend*

128.54 carats: weight of the "Fancy Yellow" Tiffany diamond in the flagship New York City store on Fifth Avenue

$7.5 million: cost to build the *Titanic* in 1912 (equal to about $400 million by today's economic standards)

15,000: size of workforce hired specifically to build the *Titanic*

$10: average weekly salary of laborers hired to build the *Titanic*

4 months: how long laborers would have needed to work in order to amass enough money to buy one First Class (berth) ticket on the *Titanic*

64: lifeboat capacity of the *Titanic* (had the ship actually been equipped with 64 lifeboats, there would have been more than enough seats for everybody on board; however, because only 16 were legally required, White Star, the owners, cut the number to 32, and then again to 20, voicing concern that too many boats "would sully the aesthetic beauty of the ship")

1: *Titanic* survivors still alive as of 2009 (Milvinia Dean of England)

2.5 miles: distance beneath the ocean's surface where the *Titanic* now lies

5,500: objects, ranging from delicate porcelain dishes to a 17-ton section of the hull, that have been rescued from the wreckage site

TITANIC

8 million lbs.: sugar used to make the 500 million Twinkies that Interstate Bakeries sells every year

39: ingredients in a single Twinkie (counting the vitamins and minerals in the fortified flour)

$.05: price of the Twinkie 2-pack when it was introduced in 1930 (the original filling was banana; it was replaced by vanilla-flavored cream during WWII, when the U.S. experienced a banana shortage)

10 minutes: time it takes to bake a Twinkie

45 seconds: average time it takes a Twinkie to explode in a microwave

25 days: official shelf life of a Twinkie

VW BEETLE

2: words used in the ad campaign to launch the VW Beetle ("Think small")

$1,480: price tag on the first VW Beetle in 1949

71mph: top speed of the first Beetle

53: racing number of "Herbie," the VW Beetle featured in the Disney movie series *The Love Bug*

21,529,464: total VW Beetles produced as of May 2003 (when production ceased on the original model), making it the most produced car model of all time

$23,000: amount paid at auction for the VW Beetle that appeared on the cover of The Beatles' *Abbey Road* album

555 feet, 5 1/8 inches: height of the Washington Monument (by law, no other building in D.C. is allowed to be taller)

152 feet: point on the monument (going from the ground up) where the color of the marble blocks changes slightly (due to the switch in building materials, from Maryland marble to a darker-toned Massachusetts marble, after a 22-year hiatus in construction)

36,491: blocks in the Washington Monument

897: stairs to the top of the Washington Monument

75 years: length of time after the Washington Monument was completed before an elevator was installed (it now takes 70 seconds to get to the top)

30 miles: distance visible from the top of the Washington Monument

$15 million: the cost to build 3 granite security walls around the Washington Monument in 2005, prompted by 9/11

WASHINGTON MONUMENT

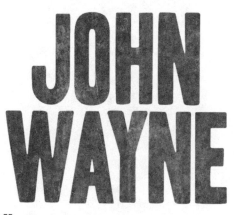

JOHN WAYNE

13 lbs.: weight of John Wayne at birth

142: movies, out of the 175 he made, where John Wayne was the lead (more lead roles than any other actor)

8: John Wayne movies in which his character died

23: times that John Wayne addressed Jimmy Stewart as "pilgrim" in *The Man Who Shot Liberty Valence* (although this would become a standard line in any impersonation of John Wayne, the actor only used the term in one other film, *McLintock!*, and then only once)

5: packs of Camel cigarettes John Wayne smoked per day

0: times, since the inception of the Harris poll of America's Favorite Film Stars in 1994, that John Wayne has been out of the top ten (especially impressive in light of the fact that Wayne died in 1979)

2: awards given to John Wayne by the U.S. government—the Congressional Gold Medal (in 1979) and the Presidential Medal of Freedom (posthumously, in 1980)

168 feet: length of the White House

570: gallon cans of paint required to paint the outside surface of the White House

18 acres: land enclosed by the White House fence

1015: square footage of the Oval Office

35: bathrooms in the White House

WHITE

5,000: daily visitors to the White House

5: chefs on staff at the White House (able, if needed, to serve dinner to as many as 140 guests at one time)

1: number of 2008 holiday ornaments created especially for the White House—by an artist in each of the country's 435 congressional districts—that were deemed too controversial to display (a 9-inch ball from Seattle's 7th Congressional District that said "Impeach Bush")

HOUSE

200: entries posted on Wikipedia within one month of launching on January 15, 2001

2.6 million: approximate entries (in English) posted on Wikipedia as of January 15, 2009

75,000: anonymous contributors and editors to Wikipedia

2: percentage of Wikipedia's contributors responsible for 73.4% of the Web site's edits

10 million: edits to Wikipedia entries posted daily

1: rank of Wikipedia in the list of the top 3,200 educational reference sites in the U.S., according to Hitwise data

$580 million: estimated market value of Wikipedia, if the non-profit Web site were to run ads

22 inches: height of Winnie-the-Pooh

100: acres in "The Wood" where Pooh, Eeyore, Piglet, Tigger, Kanga, and Roo live

50: languages, including Latin, into which *Winnie-the-Pooh* and *House at Pooh Corner* have been translated since 1928 (the Latin edition—called *Winnie ille Pu*—became the first foreign-language book to make *The New York Times* Bestseller List)

2: streets that have been named after Winnie-the-Pooh (one is in Warsaw, the other in Budapest)

750,000: people who annually visit the original stuffed Winnie-the-Pooh (and his friends) in the Central Children's Room at the Donnell Library Center in the New York Public Library

$6 billion: income the Winnie-the-Pooh franchise generates for the Walt Disney Company yearly (more than is earned by Mickey Mouse, Minnie Mouse, Donald Duck, Goofy, and Pluto combined)

$2 million: amount paid at Sotheby's in London on December 17, 2008, for a series of original Winnie-the-Pooh drawings by E. H. Shepard

Winnie-the-Pooh

The Wizard
of OZ
(1939)

5: directors that it took to bring *The Wizard of Oz* to the screen

$50: salary paid, for a 6-day work week, to the actors who portrayed the Munchkins

$125: salary paid to Toto the dog per work week

$75,000: offer MGM made to W.C. Fields to play the Wizard (Fields turned down the role to devote his time to writing the script for *You Can't Cheat an Honest Man*)

9 days: time after filming began that Buddy Ebsen (who had been cast as the Tin Man) suffered an allergic reaction to the aluminum powder makeup he wore, was hospitalized, and had to be replaced by Jack Haley (Haley was never told the reason why and Ebsen's vocals can be heard whenever *We're off to see the Wizard* is played)

The Wizard of OZ

(continued)

35 foot: length of the muslin stocking used as the tornado in the film (it was photographed over a miniature of a Kansas farm and fields)

5 1/2: size of the ruby slippers Dorothy wore

90 lbs.: weight of the Cowardly Lion's costume

3: lines of dialogue from *The Wizard of Oz* that made the American Film Institute's list of the 100 Greatest Movie Lines of all time ("Toto, I have a feeling we're not in Kansas anymore'"; "There's no place like home"; "I'll get you, my pretty, and your little dog, too")

1: where *Over the Rainbow* ranks on the American Film Institute's list of the 100 Greatest Movie Songs of all time

32: musical acts that performed at Woodstock (first in the lineup was Richie Havens)

4: acts who were slated to appear at Woodstock but cancelled (Joni Mitchell, Jeff Beck Group, Iron Butterfly, and Lighthouse)

25: songs in the set performed by the Who (the most of any act)

1: gigs Crosby, Stills, Nash, and Young had played before their Woodstock performance

WOODSTOCK FESTIVAL

200: arrests on site at Woodstock (out of 500,000 people in attendance)

2: deaths at Woodstock (one person died of a drug overdose and one was run over by a tractor while sleeping in a field)

2: births at Woodstock

$0: cost to get into Woodstock (while tickets were originally priced at $6-$8/day, early on the crowd tore down the fence enclosing the festival grounds and everyone was admitted for free)

$1.3 million: estimated profits the promoters lost by not being able to charge all of those in attendance